I C O

History Ma

Martin
Luther King, Jr.

by Pamela McDowell

MEDIA ENHANCED BOOKS
AV²
BY WEIGL™
ADDED VALUE • AUDIO VISUAL

www.av2books.com

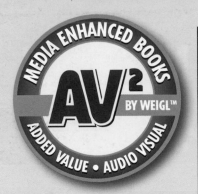

AV² provides enriched content that supplements and complements this boo
Weigl's AV² books strive to create inspired learning and engage young min
in a total learning experience.

Your AV² Media Enhanced books come alive with...

Audio
Listen to sections of
the book read aloud.

Key Words
Study vocabulary, and
complete a matching
word activity.

Video
Watch informative
video clips.

Quizzes
Test your knowledge.

Go to **www.av2books.com**,
and enter this book's
unique code.

BOOK CODE

W402007

Embedded Weblinks
Gain additional information
for research.

Slide Show
View images and
captions, and prepare
a presentation.

AV² by Weigl brings you media
enhanced books that support
active learning.

Try This!
Complete activities and
hands-on experiments.

... and much, much mor

Published by AV² by Weigl
350 5th Avenue, 59th Floor
New York, NY 10118

www.av2books.com   www.weigl.com

Copyright ©2014 AV² by Weigl

Library of Congress Cataloging-in-Publication Data

McDowell, Pamela.
 Martin Luther King, Jr. / Pamela McDowell.
   pages cm. -- (Icons)
 ISBN 978-1-62127-309-7 (hardcover : alk. paper) -- ISBN 978-1-62127-
315-8 (softcover : alk. paper)
1. King, Martin Luther, Jr., 1929-1968--Juvenile literature. 2. African
American civil rights workers--Biography--Juvenile literature. 3. African
Americans--Civil rights--History--20th century--Juvenile literature. I.
Title.
 E185.97.K5M35 2013
 323.092--dc23
 [B]
                      2013000835

Printed in the United States of America in North Mankato, Minnesota
1 2 3 4 5 6 7 8 9 0 17 16 15 14 13

WEP040413
052013

Editor: Megan Cuthbert
Design: Tammy West

Photograph Credits
Weigl acknowledges Getty Images as the primary image supplier for
this title. Every reasonable effort has been made to trace ownership and
to obtain permission to reprint copyright material. The publishers would
be pleased to have any errors or omissions brought to their attention so
that they may be corrected in subsequent printings.

Contents

"Non-violence is a powerful and just weapon which cuts without wounding and ennobles the man who wields it. It is a sword that heals."

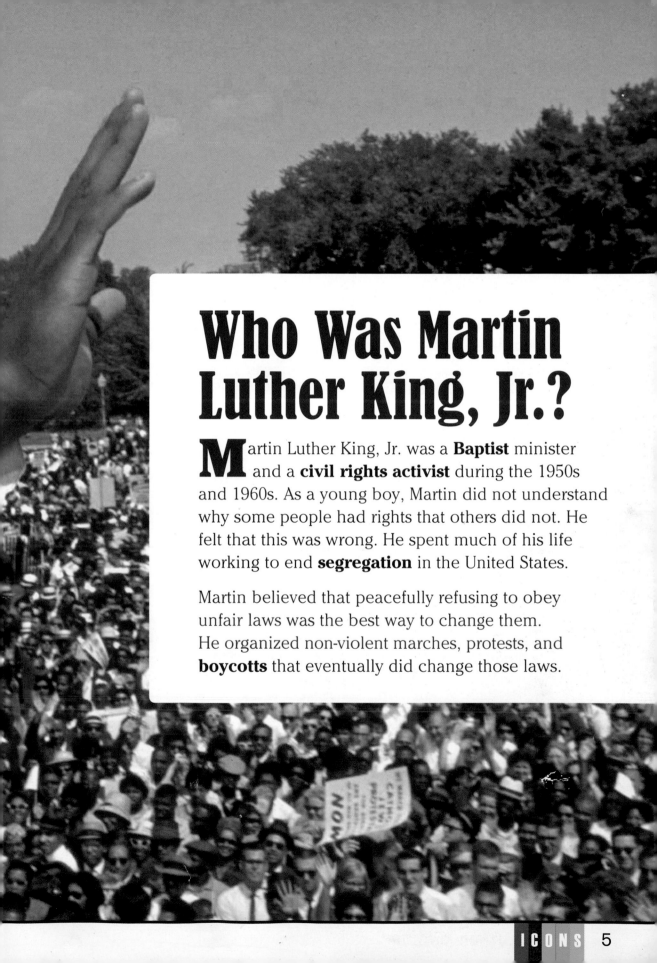

Who Was Martin Luther King, Jr.?

Martin Luther King, Jr. was a **Baptist** minister and a **civil rights activist** during the 1950s and 1960s. As a young boy, Martin did not understand why some people had rights that others did not. He felt that this was wrong. He spent much of his life working to end **segregation** in the United States.

Martin believed that peacefully refusing to obey unfair laws was the best way to change them. He organized non-violent marches, protests, and **boycotts** that eventually did change those laws.

Growing Up

Michael King, Jr. was born January 15, 1929, in Atlanta, Georgia. His father was a Baptist minister. Like his father, Michael changed his name to honor the German religious leader, Martin Luther. Young Martin attended Booker T. Washington High School in Atlanta. He was an excellent student and was allowed to skip grades nine and eleven.

Martin Luther King, Sr. and his wife, Alberta, protected young Martin and his sister and brother from the hurtful effects of segregation. In 1944, Martin and his teacher were riding a bus home from a speech contest. Martin was angry when he was told to give up his seat for the white people boarding the bus. He was young, but he recognized the unfairness of segregation.

▲ Segregation laws separated African Americans from other Americans in public places such as theaters, restaurants, and schools.

Get to Know Georgia

NORTH CAROLINA

SOUTH CAROLINA

ATLANTIC OCEAN

ALABAMA

GEORGIA

N

SCALE

0   50 Miles

0   50 Kilometers

The Georgia State Capitol, in Atlanta, was completed in 1889. The dome at the center of the building has gold leaf that was mined in Dahlonega, Georgia.

The 1996 Summer Olympics took place in Atlanta.

Georgia is nicknamed the "Peach State." The state is known for growing high quality peaches.

The state capital of Georgia is Atlanta, which is the largest city in the state. In 2010, more than 420,000 people lived in Atlanta. More than 5 million people live in the Atlanta **metropolitan** area.

STATE SYMBOLS

TREE
Live Oak

BIRD
Brown Thrasher

FLOWER
Cherokee Rose

Practice Makes Perfect

Martin entered Morehouse College in Atlanta when he was 15 years old. After graduating with a degree in **sociology**, he attended Crozer Theological Seminary in Chester, Pennsylvania. At Crozer, Martin studied religion, with the goal of becoming a minister. He graduated at the top of his class. He later completed a **Ph.D.** in **theology** at Boston University.

While he was away at school, Martin wrote a letter to the editor of the *Atlanta Constitution* newspaper. In his letter, he said that African Americans should have the same rights as all American citizens. This letter was one of Martin's first steps as a civil rights activist.

▲ Martin was pastor of the Dexter Avenue Baptist Church from 1954 to 1960. His role at the church made him an important voice for the community.

In 1953, Martin married Coretta Scott. They moved to Montgomery, Alabama, where Martin became a pastor. As a pastor, he further developed his skill at delivering speeches.

The direction of Martin's life changed on December 1, 1955, when a woman he did not know, Rosa Parks, was arrested in Montgomery, Alabama. Rosa Parks was tired after a long day of work and refused to give up her seat on a public bus to a white man. She was arrested for her **civil disobedience**.

The night Rosa Parks was arrested, Martin was selected to lead a bus boycott. The African American citizens of Montgomery refused to ride the bus until the law was changed. The boycott succeeded. After 382 days of protest, racial segregation on Montgomery buses ended.

QUICK FACTS

- When he was 10, Martin sang with his church choir at the Atlanta premier of the movie *Gone With the Wind.*

- There are more than 730 streets in the United States named after Martin.

- Martin's father, grandfather, and great grandfather were all Baptist ministers.

◀ In November, 1956, the Supreme Court ruled that bus segregation was illegal, and the Montgomery Bus Boycott ended. A month later, Rosa Parks was riding on a bus that was no longer segregated.

Key Events

The Montgomery Bus Boycott in 1955 was Martin's first non-violent civil rights protest. In May 1957, he led more than 25,000 people to Washington, D.C., in the Prayer **Pilgrimage** for Freedom. This was the largest civil rights protest Americans had seen. Martin gave his first national **address** when the group arrived in Washington, D.C.

Support for Martin grew. He lectured all over the United States on topics of segregation and equality. On August 28, 1963, Martin led the March on Washington for Jobs and Freedom. The march attracted more than 200,000 protestors. Here, he gave his most famous speech, "I Have a Dream," which described his hope for all people to live together as equals. This 17-minute speech brought segregation to the attention of the entire country and increased the pressure on government to change the laws.

Martin received the Nobel Prize for Peace on December 10, 1964. At the time, he was the youngest person to receive the prize. Winning the award helped bring worldwide attention and even more support for Martin's cause.

◄ Martin delivered his "I Have A Dream" speech to an enormous crowd. The speech was also televised and broadcast to an audience of millions.

Thoughts from Martin

Martin was a powerful public speaker who used his speeches to convince others to join the civil rights movement. Here are some of comments he has made about his efforts.

Martin talks about faith.
"Faith is taking the first step even when you don't see the whole staircase."

Martin's thoughts on the importance of justice.
"Injustice anywhere is a threat to justice everywhere."

Martin believes he has to continue his struggle for equal civil rights.
"I have begun the struggle and I can't turn back. I have reached the point of no return."

Martin explains why he believes in non-violence as a way of creating change.
"Darkness cannot drive out darkness: only light can do that. Hate cannot drive out hate: only love can do that."

Martin writes about the danger of remaining silent when something is wrong.
"We will have to repent in this generation not merely for the hateful words and actions of the bad people but for the appalling silence of the good people."

One of Martin's most famous speeches is "I Have a Dream."
"I have a dream that my four little children will one day live in a nation where they will not be judged by the color of their skin but by the content of their character."

What Is a Civil Rights Activist?

A civil rights activist fights against laws that are unfair. He or she is a leader dedicated to creating equal opportunity for members of a **minority group**. A civil rights activist will point out an inequality and demand change.

Civil rights leaders are often skilled speakers who are able to motivate and inspire people. Protests, marches, and boycotts are most successful when many people participate. An activist may choose to go on a hunger strike. Refusing to eat is a non-violent way to draw attention to a cause.

Civil rights activists often become the focus of anger and frustration. They may be threatened and physically harmed. They may be arrested and spend years in jail. Some civil rights activists are often in danger of being **assassinated**.

PROTEST

A person or group will protest if they disagree with something, usually a decision by a company or government, or a law. A person can protest by themselves or gather a large group. The aim of a protest is to change the situation the protestors disagree with. To achieve change, a protest must raise awareness of the cause. Protestors will often meet in a public place and carry large signs. They hope that the public will be convinced to join the cause. Protests are usually most effective when many people support it. This way, there is more pressure on a government or company to change the law or decision.

Civil Rights Activists 101

Nelson Mandela (1918–)

Rolihlahla Mandela was born in Transkei, South Africa. When he began school, he was given the name Nelson by his teacher. Nelson joined the African National Congress and led South Africans in the protest to end **apartheid**. He was arrested and sentenced to life imprisonment in 1964. The government eventually released Nelson in 1990. In 1994, Nelson was elected South Africa's first black president. Nelson was awarded the Nobel Prize for Peace in 1993.

Ruby Bridges (1954–)

Ruby Bridges was born in Tylertown, Mississippi. At the age of six, she became the first African American child to attend an all-white elementary school in the South. Federal marshals accompanied Ruby to school where she was met by an angry mob. Only one teacher agreed to teach Ruby. That first year, Ruby learned her lessons alone with her teacher. By grade 2, Ruby had joined other students in her class.

Tawakkol Karman (1979–)

Tawakkol Karman was born in Taiz, Yemen. She is a mother and journalist who started a group called "Women Journalists Without Chains." Since 2007, she has organized weekly protests against the Yemeni government, demanding it recognize basic human rights and women's rights. She has been arrested and imprisoned twice. Tawakkol is sometimes called the "mother of the revolution" and "the iron woman." In 2011, she was awarded the Nobel Prize for Peace with two other female peacemakers.

Malala Yousafzai (1997–)

Malala Yousafzai was born in Mingora, Pakistan, in an area that was controlled by the **Taliban**. The Taliban banned girls from attending school. Malala's father, Ziauddin, ran a school for girls. From a young age, Malala knew that education was important. She spoke out against the Taliban's restrictions on women's education. In 2012, a Taliban gunman attempted to assassinate Malala. She survived the attack, but faced many months of recovery. In 2013, Malala was nominated for the Nobel Peace Prize.

Influences

Martin never met the person who was one of the greatest influences on his life. Mahatma Gandhi was an Indian civil rights activist who dedicated his life to non-violent protest. He encouraged people to resist the government using non-violent civil disobedience. Gandhi worked to improve women's rights, end poverty, and free India from British control. He wanted to change the laws in India and bring freedom to his people. He was successful, although he was also threatened, arrested, and eventually assassinated.

Gandhi's beliefs were first brought to Martin's attention at Morehouse College by Howard Thurman. Howard was a **missionary** and teacher who had met Gandhi. Bayard Rustin was another important influence on Martin. He was a well-known activist who had also studied Gandhi's methods of creating change. As one of Martin's advisors, he helped to persuade Martin to follow Gandhi's principles of non-violence.

◀ **Gandhi lived in South Africa for several years and worked toward improving conditions for Indians there. He then returned to his home country to continue fighting for equality for his people.**

Martin visited Gandhi's birthplace in 1959. He felt a strong connection to the civil rights activist. He left India determined to free his people from the unfair laws of segregation. Martin hung a portrait of Gandhi in the family's dining room as a constant reminder of his goal.

THE KING FAMILY

Martin and his wife Coretta had four children, Yolanda, Martin Luther King III, Dexter Scott, and Bernice. Martin spent much of his time traveling around the country, giving speeches and leading marches. Coretta supported his beliefs. She marched with her husband when she could and raised their children while he was away.

▲ Just two weeks after Martin's first child, Yolanda, was born, he began the Montgomery Bus Boycott.

Overcoming Obstacles

Martin was committed to peaceful protest as a way to change laws. These changes threatened the way many people had lived for a very long time. They often reacted with violence. Martin's home was bombed while his family was inside, and he received death threats.

A peaceful demonstration in downtown Birmingham, Alabama, in 1963, ended badly. The city police turned dogs loose on the crowd and sprayed the protesters with fire hoses. Martin and others were sent to jail for their disobedience.

◀ Martin was arrested a total of 30 times. Most of his arrests were the result of ignoring segregation laws.

▲ On March 30, 1965, Coretta Scott King helped her husband lead the march from Selma to Montgomery. It took five days to complete and covered 54 miles (87 kilometers).

On March 7, 1965, a march was organized from Selma to Montgomery, Alabama. It ended violently when angry mobs and the police attacked the demonstrators. The day was named Bloody Sunday. Martin was not at that march, but he responded to the violence immediately. He organized a peaceful protest on March 9 and again on March 25. Many younger people were becoming frustrated. They saw Martin's non-violent way of protesting as weak. Despite their criticism, Martin remained firm in his belief that non-violent protest was the only way to create positive change.

Achievements and Successes

Martin was a strong family man and well-respected minister. He was determined to follow Gandhi's non-violent method of protest. His first success came when the Montgomery Bus Boycott ended in 1956. A federal court declared that the law segregating bus passengers was unconstitutional. Black citizens no longer had to ride at the back of the bus or give up their seats to white passengers.

Soon, people across the United States heard about Martin's work for equal rights. His speeches were broadcast on radio and television. More people were joining Martin's cause, and politicians could no longer ignore them. Slowly, laws began to change. In 1964, Martin was invited to witness the signing of the Civil Rights Act. The act made it illegal to **discriminate** against minorities in jobs, education, or transportation. Then, in 1965, the Voting Rights Act was passed. This act clearly stated that all citizens, including African Americans, had the right to vote. Martin had worked hard to achieve these changes. Through peaceful protests and powerful speeches, he had encouraged Americans to demand these laws from the government.

OUT OF THE MOUNTAIN OF DESPAIR, A STONE OF HOPE

◄ The Martin Luther King, Jr. Memorial in Washington, D.C., was dedicated on August 28, 2011. Martin is the first African American to receive a memorial along the National Mall.

On April 4, 1968, Martin was assassinated in Memphis, Tennessee. During his life and after his death, Martin received numerous honorary degrees from colleges and universities in the United States and around the world. In 1970, Martin was **posthumously** awarded the Grammy Award for Best Spoken Word Recording for the recording of his speech "Why I Oppose the War in Vietnam." Today, Martin Luther King, Jr. Day is a national holiday celebrated on the third Monday of January.

HELPING OTHERS

Martin spent most of his life working to eliminate inequality, poverty, and violence in order to improve the lives of all Americans. After his death, Coretta Scott King created The Martin Luther King, Jr. Center for Nonviolent Social Change in Atlanta, Georgia. The King Center educates and inspires visitors to continue Martin's work for equality for people around the world. Nearly one million people visit the King Center each year.

▶ Martin's message of equality and non-violence is promoted through events organized on Martin Luther King, Jr. Day.

Write a Biography

A person's life story can be the subject of a book. This kind of book is called a biography. Biographies describe the lives of remarkable people, such as those who have achieved great success or have done important things to help others. These people may be alive today, or they may have lived many years ago. Reading a biography can help you learn more about a remarkable person.

At school, you might be asked to write a biography. First, decide who you want to write about. You can choose a civil rights activist, such as Martin Luther King, Jr., or any other person. Then, find out if your library has any books about this person. Learn as much as you can about him or her. Write down the key events in this person's life. What was this person's childhood like? What has he or she accomplished? What are his or her goals? What makes this person special or unusual?

A concept web is a useful research tool. Read the questions in the following concept web. Answer the questions in your notebook. Your answers will help you write a biography.

Your Opinion

- What did you learn from the books you read in your research?
- Would you suggest these books to others?
- Was anything missing from these books?

Childhood

- Where and when was this person born?
- Describe his or her parents, siblings, and friends.
- Did this person grow up in unusual circumstances?

Adulthood

- Where does this individual currently reside?
- Does he or she have a family?

Writing a Biography

Main Accomplishments

- What is this person's life's work?
- Has he or she received awards or recognition for accomplishments?
- How have this person's accomplishments served others?

Work and Preparation

- What was this person's education?
- What was his or her work experience?
- How does this person work; what is or was the process he or she uses or used?

Help and Obstacles

- Did this individual have a positive attitude?
- Did he or she receive help from others?
- Did this person have a mentor?
- Did this person face any hardships?
- If so, how were the hardships overcome?

Timeline

YEAR	MARTIN LUTHER KING, JR.	WORLD EVENTS
1929	Martin Luther King, Jr. is born.	Mother Teresa begins her work among India's poorest and most diseased people.
1953	Martin marries Coretta Scott in Marion, Alabama.	The first bus boycott to protest segregation occurs in Baton Rouge, Louisiana.
1954	Martin becomes pastor of Dexter Avenue Baptist Church in Montgomery, Alabama.	The Dodgers become the first major league baseball team to have a majority of black players.
1955	The Montgomery Bus Boycott begins on December 5.	E. Frederic Morrow becomes the first African American to hold an executive position at the White House.
1963	Martin leads 250,000 people in the March on Washington and delivers his "I Have a Dream" speech.	President John F. Kennedy is assassinated.
1964	Martin receives the Nobel Prize for Peace in December.	President Lyndon B. Johnson signs the Civil Rights Act of 1964, making discrimination illegal.
1968	On April 4, Martin is assassinated in Memphis, Tennessee.	President Johnson signs the Fair Housing Act of 1968, outlawing discrimination in the sale and rental of housing.

Key Words

address: a speech

apartheid: a system of racial separation in South Africa that was enforced by the government from 1948 to 1994

assassinated: when an important person is murdered

Baptist: a part of the Protestant religion that believes in baptism of only voluntary, adult believers

boycotts: when people decide to stop using, buying, or doing something as a form of protest

civil disobedience: refusing to obey laws, usually through non-violent methods

civil rights activist: a person who tries to achieve equal rights for all citizens

discriminate: to be prejudiced against someone or something that is different

metropolitan: part of a bigger city

minority group: a small group of people who are different from most of the population

missionary: a person sent by a church to spread its religious beliefs

Ph.D.: short for Doctor of Philosophy, it is the highest degree awarded for graduate study

pilgrimage: a journey or quest made by a group of people

posthumously: happening after someone's death

segregation: the separation of African Americans from the rest of society

sociology: the study of how humans act with each other and society

Taliban: a Muslim group that follows strict religious laws

theology: the study of religion and the nature of God

Index

Log on to www.av2books.com

AV² by Weigl brings you media enhanced books that support active learning. Go to www.av2books.com, and enter the special code found on page 2 of this book. You will gain access to enriched and enhanced content that supplements and complements this book. Content includes video, audio, weblinks, quizzes, a slide show, and activities.

AV² Online Navigation

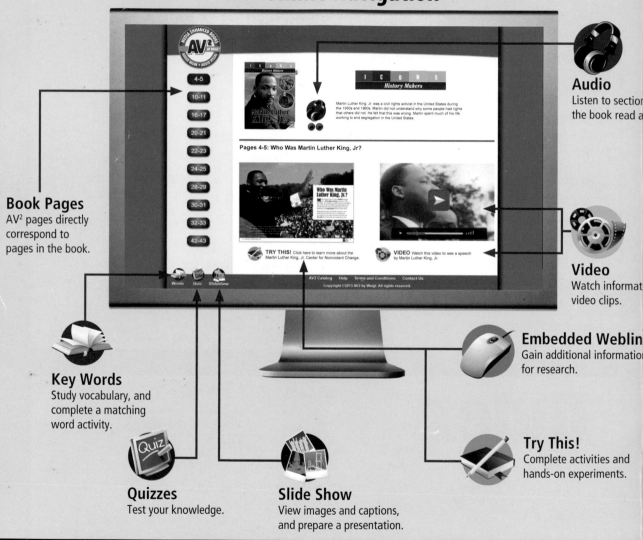

Audio
Listen to section
the book read a

Book Pages
AV² pages directly correspond to pages in the book.

Video
Watch informat
video clips.

Key Words
Study vocabulary, and complete a matching word activity.

Embedded Weblin
Gain additional information for research.

Try This!
Complete activities and hands-on experiments.

Quizzes
Test your knowledge.

Slide Show
View images and captions, and prepare a presentation.

AV² was built to bridge the gap between print and digital. We encourage you to tell us what you like and what you want to see in the future.

Sign up to be an AV² Ambassador at www.av2books.com/ambassador.